GUIDELINES FOR BOOK CATALOGS

Book Catalogs Committee
Resources and Technical Services Division
American Library Association

American Library Association

Chicago 1977

Library of Congress Cataloging in Publication Data

American Library Association. Book Catalogs Committee.
Guidelines for book catalogs.

Bibliography: p.
1. Catalogs, Book. I. Title.
Z695.87.A53   1976   025.3   77-1240
ISBN 0-8389-3190-1

Printed in the United States of America

Contents

Preface

Book catalogs in their present variety of printed, photographic, and computerized forms have been with us for only a decade or two. They have become prevalent in a variety of situations, particularly in library systems where a relatively large number of copies of the catalog are needed to service patrons at separate locations.

The Book Catalogs Committee of the Resources and Technical Services Division of the American Library Association, in line with its charter "to consider all aspects of book catalogs which fall in the area of responsibility of the Division," published a listing of active book form catalogs in the summer 1970 issue of *Library Resources and Technical Services*. The present publication is a further reaction to what the Committee saw as a need based on the many letters received from interested librarians and directors of library systems. It also functions as a teaching aid both on the formal library school level and on the informal personal interest level.

The efforts which eventuated in this publication were begun about 1971 while Joseph A. Rosenthal was the chairperson of the Committee. These efforts were continued and brought to fruition during my term as chairperson. Committee members who also shared in the work during its various phases include Ann Braithwaite, Robert Breyfogle, Barbara J. Campbell, John Corbin, Mary Kay Daniels Ganning, Allen J. Hogden, Marilyn Lamar, Alfred H. Lane, Catherine MacQuarrie, Sylvia Von Oberleithner, Jean M. Peck, Josephine Pulsifer, and Shula Schwartz. Editing assistance was graciously provided by Harris Monroe.

Joseph L. Fuchs

1

Introduction

These guidelines are written for those of you who are or will be considering a book catalog for the bibliographic representation of all or part of your library's collection, in hard copy or microfilm, or for the collections of your library system. The guidelines are intended as a road map of factors to be considered in choosing whether and how to produce a book catalog. They are not intended to describe a "model" book catalog, nor will they answer all the questions to be faced in producing one. They are designed to insure that you are acquainted with significant options and possibilities in the design and preparation of book catalogs, and to alert you to avoidable pitfalls. *Purpose of the Guidelines*

A book catalog seldom is a straightforward choice. Basic considerations, among them desirability, purpose, design, methodology, and cost, are interrelated. Tentative decisions made in one of these areas may need to be reevaluated as information is developed and possibilities clarified in others.

Is a book catalog desirable in your situation? This is obviously a basic question, and should be raised not only at the outset but repeatedly during any planning which follows. Desirability may be based on one or (usually) a combination of the following considerations: *Why a Book Catalog?*

1. The need to provide bibliographical information at multiple physical locations. Book catalogs can be duplicated and disseminated so that the collection(s) represented may be more effectively or more intensively used.
2. Preservation of existing and future bibliographical information relevant to the collection(s). This information is ordinarily contained in the present card catalog, but may be in other, special files. The book catalog as a preservation device might serve as a counteraction to the inevitable deterioration resulting from use and atmospheric conditions; it may stand as insurance against

natural or accidental disaster; and it may likewise guard against the possibility of purposeful multilation or destruction.

3. No short-term monetary saving is likely with a change from card to book catalog. There may, however, be long-range fiscal advantages—in some cases when compared to current and projected expenditures for maintenance of card files, in others only when the additional facilities and services realized through a book catalog are translated into dollar equivalencies.

Decision Factors   In almost every library system, current and anticipated costs of maintaining card catalogs should be determined, with close specification of the constituent parts. Information about cost, and cost comparison, while often not the decisive factor in the choice, design, and methodology of a book catalog, should be known as precisely as possible, and utilized during book catalog planning. The decision to produce a book catalog may provide the opportunity to present bibliographic data in more advantageous form, or through more access points (in addition to multiple physical locations) than has been the practice with a card catalog. Some of the choices available involve cataloging rules and subject analysis practice (with the possibility of an increased number of added and/or subject entries), filing arrangements, divided as opposed to dictionary files, and format and typography designed to distinguish and to clarify various data elements and types of entries. These choices are not intrinsic to the book catalog format, nor are they necessarily facilitated by all types of book catalogs. A photographic reproduction in book form of existing card files, for example, offers relatively little chance for extensive change in the presentation of bibliographic data (except at high editorial cost). The conversion of such data to machine-readable form, on the other hand, often extends the options for information display. These options, at least theoretically possible even in a card catalog system, should not be the basis of choosing a book catalog, but their practical availability in certain types of book catalog systems should not be overlooked.

Basic Purposes   The basic purposes of a book catalog will usually differ little from those of a card catalog, although the extent to which they may be realized under one system as opposed to another may vary to a great degree. Consideration of a book catalog should involve examination, or reexamination, of the underlying purposes of bibliographical representation so that the system chosen should most effectively satisfy those purposes:

1. To enable a user to ascertain whether or not a given item is in the collection and, if so, to indicate how the user may retrieve the item
2. To display, in appropriate relationship, works of like authorship and works relating to the same subject
3. To distinguish different editions or versions of the same work in the collection.

These purposes are not necessarily incompatible, but they *are* different; the degree to which each is emphasized or provided for should be explicitly realized in terms of the particular collection, library, or library system. *Such emphasis will have a direct bearing on the services provided by the resultant catalog and its cost.* Format is immaterial to the traditional rationale for a library catalog. In practical terms, choice depends on the relative functional importance of the catalog as (1) a finding list and (2) a bibliographical tool. This emphasis should be determined through careful analysis and weighing of the following considerations:

1. The nature and size of the collection
2. The uses to which the collection is put and the recognized characteristics of the users
3. The necessity or desirability for refinement of the bibliographical detail and for the precise identification of items in the collection.

These considerations, vital to the overall nature and composition of the catalog, will help determine most of the detailed specifications. For example, the basic methodology, type size, manner of supplementation, alphabetization, and binding of a book catalog representing a rare book or manuscript collection (for which the book catalog may serve as a prestigious inducement for further donations) may be at complete variance with the parallel features of a catalog representing the juvenile collections within a multilibrary county system (where a major purpose is to encourage wide use of the available resources and to inform potential users of additions to those resources.)

Scope   Each library system must determine the bibliographical items to be represented in the book catalog. This determination, of course, is intimately related to the purposes and desirability of the catalog, and will have direct implications for design, format, method of production, and cost.

Cataloging *Standards*   Consistent standards and practices of cataloging are vital in the production of book catalogs. A card catalog is generally not distributed and a reference staff, well acquainted with the eccentricities of the file, is usually able to guide users through inconsistent cataloging practices developed over a period of time. A book catalog is distributable and instructions for its use are usually provided in writing, with the catalog itself. The finished product should have few or no deviations from the published instructions.

Editing *Bibliographic* *Data*   Since discrepancies do exist in a card catalog, editing requirements can become quite complex. If all bibliographical data are input by the library producing the book catalog, cataloging rules and practices can continue to follow those applied to the retrospective files. However, if bibliographical data for additions to the collection come from another source, directly or indirectly, such as the Library of Congress MARC distribution program, a commercial firm or a library consortium with processing capability, the degree to which local practice corresponds to that followed by the cataloging data source must be scrupulously examined. Some factors to consider are: 1. What changes to data received from another source must or should be made? 2. Will names and subject headings be consistent with those already established in the local files? If not, should changes be made to incoming data, should old headings be modified, or should connecting links be formed to guide the user from old to new records and vice versa? 3. Can classification numbers provided by these outside sources be accepted without modification? 4. Has the local library in the past given extensive subject heading analysis or detailed bibliographic descriptions which are not available from these sources? If so, should these local practices be continued?

Each change to a bibliographical record costs money, no matter if it is made to a Library of Congress catalog card, a set of catalog cards from a commercial firm, or the equivalent data in a machine-readable record. Conversely, the less modification made to records received from other sources, the less the cost of processing. Before undertaking the preparation of a book catalog, the library may need to evaluate the comparatively short-run costs of changing cataloging practices (and providing bibliographical links necessary as a consequence) with the cost of continuing peculiar local practices indefinitely. In a broader sense, all this must be weighed against difficulties reference staffs and users may encounter with library catalogs which reflect a sharp change in principles and practices of bibliographical representation.

The most common reason for production of a book catalog representing one portion of a library's collection stems from the special character of the items therein, and the desirability of making them bibliographically available to a wider public than that which uses the existing card catalog. The nature of the collection may therefore serve to make the resulting book catalog attractive to other libraries and institutions with offsetting production costs. Ordinarily, however, anticipated sales should not be a major determinant in the decision to produce a book catalog. *Catalog Contents*

Because of the increasing development of library networks, almost any library considering a book catalog may have good reasons to view nearby collections as potential candidates for inclusion. Coordinated planning may be more difficult but cost-sharing may justify the additional effort. Whether the items to be represented in a book catalog form a particular collection, are the substantially complete holdings of a library, or comprise resources in two or more libraries, other decisions must usually be made:

1. Should materials other than books be included, such as serials; microforms; nonprint materials: maps, slides, films, sound recordings?

2. If the items to be represented comprise holdings in two or more physically separate buildings, or units of a library, should the book catalog reflect location of items?
3. Should the catalog include only current materials, that is, items added or published after a certain date? If a retrospective card file is maintained, then newly purchased "retrospective" materials could be entered there; the book catalog would be updated to show only newly published items.
4. Should the catalog include only retrospective materials?
5. Should the catalog include both current and retrospective items?
6. If the catalog is to include materials currently added, what provision is to be made for updating (supplements and cumulations)?

Nonbook Materials   The inclusion of bibliographical data for items other than books should be considered from various points of view:

1. What scope will best serve the users of the book catalog, and how will the inclusion of nonbook items fit in with the present and future public service operations of the library?
2. To what extent are the data for book and nonbook materials compatible?
3. Can they feasibly be merged into a single machine-readable data base?
4. If the book catalog is to be produced by photographic means, are entries and access points for both book and nonbook items such that they can be integrated in a single manual file?

Some indication of the answers to these questions may be found in the present structure of the card catalogs or other bibliographical records. If *data* for books, serials, and non-print materials *are* already in one catalog, users and staff may be accustomed to a single-file approach. It is likely too, that a single authority system exists for name and subject headings, and that common or at least compatible practices are followed with respect to descriptive cataloging. Common practices are less likely with multiple bibliographic files.

If present catalogs or other records are to be merged, of if, for future accessions, records for book and nonbook materials will form a single new data base (manual or machine), careful study is necessary to develop ground rules for data compatibility. Generally, this will be more difficult if the resultant book catalog is machine-based. Machines can neither identify nor distinguish varying kinds of bibliographical data elements or varying types of bibliographical records unless distinctions which may be "apparent" to a human being reading a catalog card are made explicit. For example, guide cards and/or filing instructions may separate works by and about Stravinsky into categories such as:

1. Scores
2. Nonmusical writing
3. Sound recordings of compositions by Stravinsky
4. Biography and criticism
5. Libretti of theatrical and operatic works for which Stravinsky composed the music
6. Dance notations of works set to Stravinsky compositions
7. Films or other visual records of productions based on his music. These categories do not necessarily appear as part of the actual bibliographical records for the physical items. In order for a computer to maintain them in a printout, appropriate identification must accompany each bibliographical record.

Serials in a book catalog deserve careful attention. Bibliographical treatment of serials with respect to card catalogs is extremely diverse: *Serials*

1. They may or may not be represented in the principal card catalogs. If they are, they may be shown under main, added, and subject entries or given only one (main or title) entry.
2. They may be included in the book classification system

followed by monographic works, shelved alphabetically by title or main entry, or given an arbitrary classification which bears little or no resemblance to that used elsewhere in the collection.

3. Volume and issue holdings for serials may or may not be reflected under the various access points given to serial titles in the card catalog.

Changing to a book catalog system gives the opportunity to reexamine present serial cataloging and recording practices and to modify both the practices and the records which are produced.

The Microform Book Catalog   Book catalogs do not necessarily have to appear in a full-size format. All the guidelines for producing book catalogs in printed form can apply to the production of a catalog in microform as well and all the same questions have to be answered. Only the format in which the final product appears will differ. Two basic situations could lead to consideration of a microform catalog:

1. There is an existing card catalog, and branch libraries are being established. You would like to have a copy of the complete card catalog in each branch (this would be true for branch libraries of a public library system or departmental libraries of a college or university system). Or you are interested in keeping an archival record of your existing card catalog. Microfilming would provide the opportunity to have a stored duplicate of the card catalog in case of catastrophe or loss by natural wear and tear.

2. You are presently producing a book catalog from machine-readable data. The printing costs are mounting, but you still have the need for multiple copies of your catalog.

Cost as a Factor   There will be some initial systems design cost in producing a microform catalog in lieu of a book catalog which could range from minimal for formatting only to a large outlay for a total systems design. If a data base is currently used for production of a book catalog, the cost of redesign should be minimal. If systems and programming help are available in your institution, the conversion cost should be relatively low. In reproducing the microform catalog, however, cost becomes a significant factor. To reproduce a one-hundred-foot reel of 16 mm microfilm containing the equivalent of twenty-five hundred pages of information currently costs about six dollars per reel for reproduction and insertion into a cartridge. Microfiche reproduction, while sometimes costing more for production of masters, costs less for duplication.

Preparing the User

When converting to a microfilm or microfiche catalog, a training program for both staff and patron must be carefully conceived. Instructions should accompany each microform reader so that the patron knows how to handle the equipment. Technicians should be trained in simple maintenance of the machinery and the user should be trained to seek help in the event of mechanical problems.

Other Guidelines

Lease or rental of microform readers should be considered so that updated versions of the equipment can be acquired as they become available in this rapidly advancing technology. Enough readers should be obtained to meet the requirements of usage at its highest peak, and to provide access to the catalog at off-site installations. When filming is completed, a master copy of the negative should be retained in case of loss or damage. Microfiche can be easily misplaced.

2

Basic Methodology

The recent resurgence of library book catalogs has seen various techniques utilized. The present discussion will concentrate on methods involving the application of advanced technology in one or more of the following areas: photography, electronic data processing (computers), computer-linked photocomposition, and offset printing. Considering the variety of photographic, computing, and printing equipment available today, an almost infinite variety of production methods is possible. Cost data given for a particular application are usually *not* transferrable to another library situation, although they may be valuable as benchmark figures in estimating costs, and will generally indicate the important cost components for the technique described.

Letterpress   Letterpress, the traditional means of producing library book catalogs in the nineteenth century, is seldom viable today. The expense of typesetting catalog data is too great. In traditional printing, the data for any given bibliographic record must be typeset for each access point—main, added, and subject entries—provided. Even with the comparatively high cost of noncomputerized typesetting and the general impracticability of preserving type slugs for more than a one-time use, typesetting could be used in certain situations:

1. When it is necessary to provide a catalog of high graphic quality, often requiring an extensive range of special type characters or the use of non-Roman alphabets (photo-offset may also satisfy this requirement)
2. In the absence of a need to provide successive cumulations of bibliographic data, for example, in the collection which no longer receives additions, or when changes may be adequately represented by supplements to the catalog

3. When the institution is able to finance letterpress production, or has equipment on hand to print its own
catalog.

    Photographic reproduction signifies the use of photo- *Photographic*
graphy to capture already existing catalog information, usu- *Reproduction*
ally on catalog cards. The resultant image becomes the master copy from which pages of a book catalog are produced
through offset printing. Two subspecies of this technique
should be distinguished: In the first, the cards are photographed singly, accompanied by a reduction in image size.
The product at this stage consists of reel film which is then
enlarged to provide black-on-white copy in the requisite
image size for master copy. After mounting in page format,
this becomes the plate for offset printing. In the second, the
cards are arranged or mounted at the beginning of the process
in what is an enlarged version of the final page format. After
photography and production of the image in the desired size,
offset printing again is employed for book production.

    Each of the above approaches is susceptible to refinement. *Condensing*
For example, elimination of white space or unwanted infor- *Data in*
mation on catalog cards (in horizontal increments) is possible *Photography*
in either. These may be done in order to reduce the total size
(and cost) of the book catalog; to eliminate distracting, obso-
lete, or unnecessary data; to improve the appearance and
scanability of the catalog; or for a combination of these
reasons. When single cards are photographed and white
space or unwanted portions of cards are to be eliminated from
the final image, the portion to be reproduced may be uniform
in size or variable. A uniform card size makes the use of a
rotary camera economically advantageous. Variation in the
size of cards to be reproduced requires manual action for each
card, at higher cost. A common device is to shingle or overlap
the cards as they are positioned before filming. This means a
layout cost greater than one in which the whole card is photographed, but cheaper book production and better appearance
may justify it.

    Photographic reproduction is subject to limitations, the *Preediting in*
most obvious being the nature of the data to be input, in this *Photography*
case catalog cards. Assuming that a corpus of cards already

exists, replacement or modification of some of the cards may be advisable, as editorial work, before the reproduction process begins. In some ways, this is analagous to the corrections and changes which catalogers make to any card catalog. However, the need for a widely disseminated book catalog which can not be cheaply or easily modified later may force the library to consider a large-scale editorial operation before photography begins. The cost and detailed methodology of such work, while not strictly a part of book catalog production, should be estimated and kept in mind as part of the total effort. (This limitation is less important in a computer-produced book catalog, where particular records or individual data elements in bibliographical records *may* be changed more easily and more cheaply).

Rehabili-
tation
of Catalog
Cards
The physical nature of the card catalog file poses other problems. Although most catalog cards conform to the standard 7.5 by 12.5 centimeter size, there are exceptions. Guide cards, for example, may have to be extracted or handled in a nonstandard manner. The physical condition of the file may range from excellent to deplorable: cards may be smudged, dog-eared, or broken, depending on length of time in the catalog, the use to which they have been put, and atmospheric conditions. In most catalogs of any size and history, different means of production and reproduction have been employed over the years and the card stock itself has probably changed. Such changes bring variations in the contrast between printed and white areas of the cards and camera adjustments are made to heighten contrast in the image to be captured. There is a corresponding decrease in resolution, and the ability to reproduce in fine detail the image on the original card. Serifs and other printing details may become indistinguishable and small size type may become illegible. Camera adjustments to strike a balance between desirable contrast and satisfactory resolution are possible on an individual card basis, but substantially increase the cost of photography. In most filming projects, a uniform setting is established, through testing, which will achieve acceptable image reproduction on both counts. The greater the variation in the original card file, however, the less likely a final product of high graphic quality.

The standard size of catalog cards imposes other restrictions on book catalog production. Generally speaking, a reduction in the image size is desirable in order to conserve space and costs. In the interest of legibility, however, photographic reduction should be limited. For those catalogs over which the Library of Congress has direct control (those for which LC prepares camera-ready copy shingled on boards), a specified reduction ratio of 42 percent has been in effect for some years. The New York Public Library, in a study preparatory to the production of its retrospective catalog in book form, called for a ratio of 40 to 45 percent. Specification of a reduction ratio directly affects the page size (or at least page width) of the book catalog. Little opportunity usually exists to trim or delete the vertical margins of cards—some cards in most files have printed or typed matter extending almost to the right or left margin or both. A specific reduction ratio, coupled with a decision as to how many columns of card images are to be mounted on a single page, will be the primary determinant of page width, with due allowance for page margin and gutter. Finally, the photographic process is limited by the nature of the original copy. Although contrast—and resultant clarity—may be increased through photography, different type or print styles cannot be changed, nor can the arrangement of data within a bibliographical record be altered. The basic (cost) advantage of photography lies in eliminating the necessity for character-by-character transcription of bibliographical data which is part of both letterpress composition or computer-based book catalog production. But it is an advantage which must be weighed against the limitations described above.

Relation of Card Size to Photographed Catalog

Computerized book catalog production offers a wide choice in method, arrangement, format, and price. In all variations, one requirement—that the bibliographical data to be represented in the book catalog be converted to machine-readable form—is consistent.

The basic variables may be outlined as follows:

Basic Questions for Computer-Based Catalogs

1. At what stage in the cataloging process are data to be converted?
2. From what source and by what means are data to be converted?

3. What identification of data elements in bibliographical records is necessary in order to produce the desired arrangement and format in the final product?
4. How is this identification to be accomplished?
5. What type of computer equipment is necessary for the required manipulation of data?
6. What equipment can produce the graphic quality for the book catalog?

These questions match the general chronological sequence of events which takes place in computer-based book catalog production. But they neither can nor should be answered in a sequential chain. A total system must be evolved which includes or rules out all the possibilities and consequences of the various options. Most systems will be planned backwards—from a determination of the desirable features of the final product within a framework of the available resources which can be committed by the library or the library system.

Timing for Conversion

If data for works already in the collection and cataloged are to be included in the book catalog, the conversion effort for these data need bear little specific relation to ongoing bibliographical processes in the sense of integration of operations. On the other hand, if the book catalog is to include current accessions, conversion of data must ordinarily occur after the content of the bibliographical record has been determined; in other words, after cataloging. Precision in detailing each step involved in the conversion process is mandatory, but depends on the method chosen for conversion and the degree to which data elements and subelements need to be identified.

Source and Method for Conversion

Are the converted bibliographical data to be derived from existing manually-produced records within the library, or should they be secured in whole or in part from an outside source? With ever-growing data banks of bibliographical records in machine-readable form, the use of external sources becomes more and more attractive. A library need not develop a conversion operation of its own, with the attendant commitment of manpower, space, and overhead. Extracting and utilizing machine-readable bibliographical information from an external source, however, is by no means simple and will require the expertise of personnel skilled in library systems work. It is also unlikely that any available data bank will correspond exactly to the bibliographical file which the local library or system wishes to convert. Decisions concerning the utility of available data files and methods of identifying pertinent bibliographical records within them demand a thorough knowledge of the library data processing scene as well as familiarity with the structure and function of catalogs and the particular library situation.

Even though use of an external data source, such as the MARC records produced by the Library of Congress, may appear justified in terms of coverage of the local file to be converted, the content and structure of the external files may or may not be suitable for the local need. For instance:

Criteria for Use of External Machine-Readable Data Bases

1. Do the records in the external file contain all the requisite bibliographical elements?
2. Are cataloging principles—choice of entry, form of heading, description and subject analysis, classification—compatible with local practice or requirements? If not, is modification of data taken from the external file practical? Should local practice and/or requirements be changed in order that data may be accepted without modification?
3. If the external source is to be used for current local accessions, will data be available promptly?
4. If a machine-readable record for a locally acquired item is not available at the time of receipt, what strategy should be used to represent it in the book catalog? Should inclusion be delayed on the exception of data receipt within an acceptably short period of time? Or should the material be cataloged locally and the resultant data integrated with the external machine-readable data base?

The answers to these questions involve close scrutiny of potential data banks and a keen appreciation of the desirable/acceptable features of the local book form catalog.

Local
Production
of a Machine-
Readable
Data Base

Production of a machine-readable set of bibliographical records without reliance on an external file can be done either by the library itself or through a contractual relationship with another organization. The latter may be a commercial firm or a data processing center associated with an academic institution or government agency. (For a discussion of the factors to be considered in this type of contractual relationship, see section 4, Library-contractor relations.) Any decision to undertake in-house conversion of bibliographical data should probably be made only when (1) there is economical access to a nearby computer facility and (2) the library has or can employ staff competent to plan and supervise the conversion effort.

Data Input
Techniques

Whether the project is in-house or external, library staff assigned to a book catalog should be acquainted with the various data input techniques. These include keypunching and optical character recognition (or optical scanning), both of which require a further (machine) conversion of the keyboarded product resulting in data on magnetic tape which can be manipulated by the computer; keyboarding devices which produce magnetic tape directly; and reactive terminal devices which provide immediate access to a computer, that is, in an on-line environment. The keypunch is a relatively inexpensive device, yet the verification required and the comparatively slow rate of input add to personnel costs. Furthermore, input of alphanumeric data encompassing a large set of characters is difficult and cumbersome. The different input devices vary as to ease of error correction and addition or deletion of data; in general, the easier and more flexible it is to make error corrections, the greater the cost. The cost of training personnel, which is direct in an in-house operation and hidden in a contractual arrangement, will also vary according to the technique chosen.

Identifi-
cation
of Data
Elements

A fundamental principle associated with machine-based bibliographical files is that any particular record should be input only once, and that various possibilities for manipulation of data and display under desired access points can be derived from the original encoding in machine-readable form. This principle depends on more explicit identification of elements within bibliographical records than in ordinary card representation. Such identification can serve multiple purposes:

1. Sequencing of records according to chosen categories and/or desired filing arrangements
2. Formatting of records to enhance visual display, particularly in a book catalog
3. Truncation of records under certain access points to save space and reduce cost.

Any machine-based bibliographical file created to produce a book catalog must rely on some kind of standard for the identification of data elements. The most widely accepted is the MARC II format for encoding monograph records. Because of the high degree of detail in MARC II encoding, its application is costly in terms of both human assignment of data element codes and of machine processing, yet the resultant data file is more likely to offer extended possibilities for sophisticated display. Decisions on the extent of data identification must be made in close conjunction with the determination of what the scope and cost of the book catalog should be.

Production of a microform catalog from an existing card catalog is relatively simple. The catalog cards are filmed in the same sequence in which they are arranged in the card catalog; the methods of reproduction of card catalogs in the introduction are basically photographic. When the cards are photographed one at a time as the initial step in production of a book catalog by means of offset printing, the resultant film can be converted for use as a microfilm catalog or it can be stripped and formed into fiche. The problems to be considered in producing a microform catalog of this kind are identical to those of producing a book catalog, except that the cost is considerably lower. But the quality will vary depending upon the quality of the cards being photographed.

The Microform Catalog

From computer-based bibliographic data files, two methods can be used to obtain a microform catalog:

Methods of Production

1. The data can be converted from its computer-based form (usually magnetic tape) and a copy printed by the com-

puter. It is then photographed and processed for microfilming and put into reel or fiche form. This is a less costly method than printing but does result in wasted space on the microfilm record. It has the advantage of allowing more frequent updates of the entire file, avoiding the necessity for supplements.

2. The newest and most effective means of producing microform catalogs is by Computer Output Microfilm (COM), which enables you to go from magnetic tape to microform directly, eliminating the printing step entirely.

Computer Output Microfilm

Most library systems will probably contract for microfilming because equipment and supplies are expensive. However, costs with a service bureau are very low, with an average one-hundred-foot reel reproducing at a cost of about three dollars per original and one dollar for extra copies, plus cartridge and mounting charges. However, when cartridges are returned for each run, the mounting cost is eliminated.

Equipment costs would probably prohibit the installation of a COM system in-house. If, however, computers exist and there are other uses for COM-produced materials, the cost might be justified.

COM Service Bureaus

Although it is recommended that a service bureau be used if there is no in-house COM capability, it is also recommended that you review the available service bureaus carefully. The COM service industry is quite unstable, with new firms continually entering the field as others depart. Careful evaluation and discussion with others using service bureaus should lead to a reliable source.

Most of today's COM service bureaus were founded specifically to perform COM services and tend to offer the limited services of recording, processing, and duplicating microfilm. Some will be able to assist the customer with consulting, systems, and programming and can suggest retrieval techniques and specific hardware, assist in program modifications, and generally guide the user over the rough spots. All service bureaus will package the film either in rolls, cartridges, or jackets.

The turnaround time required from whenever the customer hands over his tapes until the film is returned can be as short as one day or as long as a week, depending largely on the customer's remoteness from the service bureau, method of pickup and delivery of the data, and the customer's requirements. Faster turnaround may cost more.

Service bureau prices, which vary somewhat from area to area, in general are quoted on a "per frame" basis. Prices for a specific job will depend upon the following factors: *Service Bureau Costs*

1. Volume of work (machine setup costs must be amortized over the run and affect unit costs)
2. Pickup and delivery
3. Final microform required (microfiche requires more machine time for the same number of frames than roll film, and if films must be inserted into jackets, clerical costs are increased)
4. Number of duplicate copies required
5. Input tape format (printer tapes require more machine time than tapes formatted for programmed mode of operation)
6. Amount of consulting and programming assistance required
7. Computer work required
8. Type and depth of retrieval.

The type of film used for reproduction will also be a cost variant. The most expensive, but with the best quality of reproduction, is a silver halide film because the image density tends to be greater in silver-based copies. The least expensive is diazo film, which is developed by a dry ammonia process. This film permits high-speed processing (sixty to one hundred feet per minute and more). While often as high in technical quality as silver film it produces poorer contrast of opaque and transparent film areas. A third film reproduction method, still on the verge of becoming a significant breakthrough in the industry, is the dry process, heat-developed film of which Kalvar is the archetype. This film is the easiest to use and process for duplication, and the heat process permits economies of speed. Thermal or "vesicular" films are generally more expensive than diazo types and lose more resolution in reproduction than the diazo or silver. *Types of Reproduction Films*

3

Form and Format

Catalog form refers to the sequence(s) in which bibliographical records are displayed. The card catalog exhibits two basic forms:

1. A dictionary sequence in which all types of entries—main, added, title, series, subject—are interfiled
2. Divided, where two or more alphabetically arranged sequences of records are maintained, each containing one or more distinctive categories of records

The most common form of the divided catalog is that in which subject entries are in one sequence and all other entries in another, but there are a number of other forms.

If photographic reproduction is to be used for book catalog production, considerable weight should be given to carrying over the form of the existing card catalog to the book version, since to change the form would necessitate substantial separation or amalgamation of files. Where extensive editorial or rehabilitative work is necessary to make cards acceptable for photography, however, the work of interfiling or splitting files can be coupled with other preparatory tasks if a change in the form of the catalog is deemed desirable.

A book catalog based on machine-readable data gives greater flexibility in the choice of form, provided the various access points in each record (main, added, subject, title, series entries) have been precisely identified. In fact, a decision to choose one form of catalog as opposed to others is less permanent than in a photographically reproduced catalog. The costs involved are chiefly those of obtaining or devising computer programs to produce the form desired, plus the actual costs of book production. The data themselves need not be altered.

A computer-based catalog also offers wide latitude in the bibliographical information associated with each record to be displayed under each of the access poinṫs. Decisions in this area directly affect user facility on the one hand and production costs on the other. Some questions may be helpful in formulating these decisions:

Amount of Data Displayed under Various Access Points

1. Under which access point is it *essential* that the user be provided with complete bibliographical information regarding the item listed?
2. What are the data elements in the record which will provide the user with sufficient information to identify the work listed and to enable him to decide whether or not he needs the item?
3. To what extent will users need to obtain full bibliographical information for a listed item? How seriously will users be inconvenienced by having to refer from an access point under which limited data are shown to one under which the complete record is displayed?

These questions, of course, relate to the broader concept of the purpose of the catalog—whether it is to be primarily a finding list for items in the collection represented or a bibliographical source.

Full or partial display of data under various access points affects cost principally because of the increase or decrease of space required on the resulting book catalog copy and the consequent expense in paper and binding. In cases where frequent cumulations or supplements are to be produced, book production will be a major factor in the total cost picture, and should be carefully planned.

The increasing feasibility of computer-based book catalogs has heightened the attractiveness of a special variation of the divided catalog—a form commonly known as the "register"—in which full bibliographical information is displayed for each item roughly according to the sequence in which works are acquired or cataloged. When a sufficient set of machine-readable records has been accumulated, a book volume is produced in which each record has a distinctive, sequential location identification.

Register

Accompanying these register volumes, which stand as a permanent record not subject to cumulation or alteration, are various indexes which may offer access by name entries, subjects, titles, series, classification, or even other data such as language or country of imprint. Listings in the indexes give a brief record containing such elements as main entry, short title, date and/or place, series, and classification, as well as the location in the register volume of the complete bibliographical data. The indexes, unlike the register volumes, must be supplemented and/or cumulated often enough to provide adequate user access to the collections represented.

Changes in bibliographical records are reflected by a new listing of the complete citation in the register, with corresponding changes in all index entries to refer to the new location in the register. The old complete listing remains as previously displayed in the register but access points in the indexes no longer refer to it. Because of the abbreviated nature of the listings in the indexes and the elimination of the need to reprint the complete record, the total cost of a register/index system may be significantly less than that of more traditional book catalog forms.

Filing Whatever the form of the book catalog (register, divided, or dictionary), the filing arrangement of bibliographical entries is most important. If a retrospective catalog is to be photographically reproduced, costs will probably dictate retention of the existing filing arrangement unless there are strong reasons to attempt revision, or unless the form of the book catalog will be changed (e.g., divided rather than dictionary). Production of a computer-based catalog, on the other hand, will require thorough analysis of the theory and practice of existing library filing rules and necessitate creation of a format and program for machine filing. Since computers were not primarily designed for handling linguistic data, they are not capable of making the judgments required for compliance with existing filing codes without extensive and expensive programming. Because of cost, the principle of a structured catalog, and strict adherence to accepted filing codes should be abandoned. Since the printed page of a book catalog allows scanability that a card file cannot provide, a strictly alphabetical approach to filing is more economical. The general filing arrangement as well as the treatment of specific problem areas (for example, initial articles, abbreviations, numerals, initials and acronyms, names with prefixes, hyphenated words, and so on should be explained in each issue of the book catalog.

The format chosen for a book catalog will reflect the method of its production. In a book catalog produced by photographic means, many of the format characteristics will be predetermined by the typography, size, and existing format of the catalog cards reproduced.   *Format*

The font style should be clear and legible. Distracting ornamental serifs or character sets containing a mixture of thick and thin stems should be avoided, particularly if the resultant type size for some or all data is relatively small. If more than one style of font is used, they should complement one another visually.   *Type Style and Size*

Styles of type are measured in points and picas, with points normally referring to the vertical measurement of the character body and picas indicating the lateral space within entries. avoid a distracting variety of type styles. In some instances, changes in type styles and point sizes can be used effectively in place of normal paragraph indention and may allow more characters per print line. Portions of entries or headings may be printed in caps. Unless a monotype font style (that is, one in which each character occupies an equal amount of lateral space) is chosen, however, this technique tends to eat up lateral space.

Finally, in letterpress or photocomposition systems, the use of justified rather than a ragged right data margin can be used to emphasize differences between two general categories of entries, such as between main and other types of entries. Data printed in all caps using justified right margin, however, may produce unattractive intraword spacing.

The number of columns of data printed on a page is influenced by the size of the page copy, type size, and desired column width. Two or three columns are normal. However, if one portion of the catalog consists of a class number index or other entries containing relatively few characters, four or more columns may be appropriate. In determining the width   *Page Layout* of each column, the purpose of the catalog should be kept in mind—optimum scanability for a finding list may be achieved with narrow columns, whereas wide columns may provide easier readability for a catalog used as a bibliographic record and research tool. Average column widths range from 2½ to 3½ inches. To avoid a cluttered page layout, at least ⅙ inch of white space should be left between columns and at least ½ inch of white space should be used for all page margins. More white space is required between columns with ragged right margins than for those where the right margin is justified. Vertical lines between columns may be used, although some computer systems have difficulty producing a clean straight line of this type. The following are headings commonly used in book catalogs:

Column headings:	headings printed between entries within a single column
Guide words:	single word or short phrase headings printed at the top of each page as a guide to the first and/or last entry on a page
Section headings:	headings printed at the beginning of a section of the catalog indicating the purpose of the section and possibly giving the name of the catalog
Running heads:	headings which appear at the top of each page of the catalog, with the possible exception of the first page of a section containing a section heading (these give the name of the catalog and/or purpose of the section)

Inclusion of any of these heading types should be viewed in terms of their usefulness to the casual reader as well as to the regular patron. Type size for headings, with the possible exception of guide words, should be at least 1½ times the type size used for entry data. The choice of typographical style for headings is virtually limitless—an overall sense of unity and compatibility is the goal. Sufficient leading before and after all types of headings, just as between data entries should be provided to avoid cluttered pages.

Page numbers may be set at either the top or bottom. One advantage of the former is that more white space is normally desired at the top; in addition, if a running head is printed, the number may be set in the same vertical space, avoiding a shorter column. In computer-based systems, however, it is more difficult to program page numbers in alternating flush right and flush left positions at the top of pages containing running heads than to set the numbers at the bottom in a centered position.

"Permanent durable" paper should be used for book catalog volumes which are not to be superseded or replaced. Offset book pages of this type are normally in the fifty-pound range and may be opacified. For less permanent book catalogs, the paper should be strong enough to withstand normal handling and should be sufficiently opaque to minimize "bleeding" of data from one page to another. *Physical Character-istics*

Options on page size may be limited by the method used to create the catalog, particularly if photographic reproduction is employed. Within the available range of choice, page size should be considered in conjunction with the quality of data displayed, format of entries, and the manner in which the book catalog is to be housed and used. Printing costs usually increase for nonstandard page sizes.

Although white or off-white are the most common colors for book catalogs, color variations may be effective for easy iden-tification of different sections within a book catalog. Stan-dard permanent durable paper is not available in colors other than white or off-white, although special large quantity or-ders for a particular color might be negotiated.

"Permanent" book catalogs are hardbound. Those which will be superseded may be covered in vellum, coated paper bindings, or one of the newer plastics. If a case binding is used, a ⅛-inch border beyond the paper size is recom-mended; if not, the binding should be the same size as the page. For maximum durability, the signatures of the catalog volume should be sewn on tapes, although saddle stitching may be acceptable for small volumes. Regardless of volume size, however, "perfect" binding or staples are not recom-mended for permanent editions, although they may be ac-ceptable for short-term use.

Book catalog volumes should be no more than two inches thick to ease handling and durability.

Microform   The basic guidelines relating to form and format that apply to printed book catalogs will apply to microform catalogs except that when using COM reproduction, data prepared for input to the catalog data base on punched cards or magnetic tape is usually reformatted to appear in a form which the COM unit can handle. The formatting is a choice which can be made by the library. Full bibliographical data can be retained or selected data elements can be chosen to appear in the final format. The type of library and the use made of the catalog should determine the final format.

Equipment   Equipment consideration for the card catalog has usually been limited to the card catalog cabinet. Book catalogs will require consultation space and shelving for storage. The number of consulting units and storage space needed will depend on the size of the library, the number of catalogs available for use, and the location of each catalog.

The form and format of microform catalogs will sometimes depend on equipment available for viewing. The number of readers required will depend on:

1. Whether the catalog is in divided or dictionary format
2. The number of branch or departmental libraries that would need readers
3. The need for readers in the technical services areas
4. Allowance for equipment failure.

The library should shop carefully for readers, evaluating both cost and reliability. Several models should be tested simultaneously to determine both reliability and ease of use.

4

Library Relations With Catalog Producer

The book catalog may be prepared by the library's own staff; by the data processing unit of the same governmental or academic entity; by a commercial enterprise acting as consultant, contractor, service bureau, and so on; or by the library in conjunction with one of the above.

The library and the catalog producer must agree in advance on a statement of the problem and the proposed solution—objectives, milestones, anticipated procedures—which then serves as a tool for measuring progress and success. If a contract is awarded it should be supplemented by memoranda of understanding, expressing in some detail the objectives and solutions.

Any book catalog is the result of a number of interwoven considerations. The major ones, listed here, should be included in any contract or accompanying memoranda of understanding.

Major Considerations

Source of bibliographical data

Data will be supplied by the contractor from MARC tapes, by original cataloging, or both.

Data will be supplied by the library from LC cards/proof slips, or by original cataloging, or from other input sources, or from a combination of these.

Data will be organized or keyed and proofed by the contractor, or by the library, or jointly, as agreed upon in advance.

Product definition

Specifications relating to the physical characteristics of the product should include:

1. The quality and weight of the paper and its color, possibly including multiple colors in one volume

2. The covers—softbound, such as Kivar, Bristol, or the newer plastics; hardbound; or case-bound
3. Cover artwork
4. Prefatory pages and the title page.

Specifications relating to the format within the product should include:

1. Sections. If it is to be a divided, rather than dictionary, catalog, it may be author/title/subject, author–title/subject, name–title/subject, and so on, based on the coding in the system and the sort programs for a computer-based catalog. A photographically produced catalog will follow the sequence of the cards as filed or refiled for this purpose.
2. Page display, including the use of 2- or 3-column format; section headings; running headings; variant type sizes; and fonts for headings, records, subject headings, and so on.
3. Types of records in the catalog. Are monograph, serial, audiovisual records to be intermixed or separated into different catalogs or sections. Photographically produced catalogs normally follow the existing card catalog record mix.
4. The necessary completeness of records. This may range from a complete MARC type record to a minimal author-title-call number display. White space may be eliminated in a photographically produced catalog by shingling the cards rather than reproducing a fixed (minimum) number of cards to a page. A computer generated catalog may display varying amounts of data in various sections of the catalog. Such variant format might include complete bibliographic data in one section and only indexes by title and subject, for example, in other sections.

By-products

Provision should be made, if desired, for labels for spines, circulation cards and/or book pockets, circulation pockets, book pockets, and shelflist-type cards.

Price definition

The library's agreement to pay for work performed should include:

1. A statement of the duration for which the original prices are to remain in force, explicitly defined, such as for the duration of a two-year contract
2. An escalation clause based upon the United States Department of Labor Bureau of Labor Statistics consumer price index for urban wage earners and clerical workers
3. A clearly stated basis for determining prices for products, taking into consideration the total number of pages in the finished catalog; the cost of prefatory pages above a given number, including a charge for the design and/or layout of these pages; the total number of copies, perhaps with reduced prices for multiple copies; the type of covers (hardbound, case-bound, and so on) and varying cover costs, not always directly controlled by the contractor; charges for by-products and proofing products, anticipating proofing and correction costs; and charges for records reprinted in supplements which are cumulative.

Invoicing and payment

Invoices are to be presented monthly, upon product delivery, or otherwise as stipulated.

Payment is to be required as invoiced, at term of the contract, prorated per month or quarter, deferred to next fiscal year, and so forth.

Taxes

The liability of the library for taxes or other charges due should be stated unless the library is exempt from sales or use tax, in which case the exemption number must be provided to the contractor for billing purposes.

Scheduling

Timetables for the following should be specific:

1. Schedule of cutoff dates for the receipt of data from the library for a given product
2. Schedule of cutoff dates for the receipt of proofing products from the contractor
3. Delivery date for each product, for the life of the contract (this should include, where necessary, the first simple catalog, followed by cumulated or uncumulated supplements, then a cumulated annual, followed by supplements, then a biennial, and so on, according to the library's needs
4. Length of grace period for delivery of a given product.

Definition of equipment

Although equipment capability may be implied by the specifications for the catalog output, specific hardware still should be defined to assure that the type of product envisioned will be produced. Such equipment may include: the type of computer, that is, 3d generation IBM 370 or equivalent; Videocomp equipment with specific font and type face capabilities; photographic equipment; and the type of printing or reproduction equipment, again being indicative of the type of final product.

Terminating an agreement

Any contract terminates once its time period has elapsed, unless there is an option for renewal, perhaps including a price escalation clause. Termination may also occur at other times if: (1) the library fails to meet data input schedules; (2) the library fails to pay invoices as specified; (3) the contractor fails to meet product delivery dates; or (4) the contractor fails to maintain defined product quality. In such cases, written notice must be given within a specified period of the occurrence, and work performed to date must be paid for. (Another way of handling these default situations is to renegotiate the contract, or to apply penalties previously made part of the contract.)

Other considerations

Additional factors which may be considered and included times if: (1) the library fails to meet data input schedules; (2) the library fails to pay invoices as specified; (3) the contractor fails to meet product delivery dates; or (4) the contractor fails to maintain defined product quality. In such cases, written in any contract or memorandum of understanding are as follow:

Any current contract supersedes prior agreements; contract modifications must be in writing and coexecuted; no contract may be assigned without mutual consent; the contractor may be asked to guarantee that quality work be performed; length of time may be specified for the library to inspect the product quality; a definition of "error" should be stated, as well as the percentage of such errors allowable for an acceptable product; the customer may inspect the contractor's facilities upon request; obligations are not binding in situations legally definable as an "act of God."

Before the final printing of the book catalog, at least one major proofreading of sample pages will be necessary as a check for quality and content. Photographically produced catalog pages will need to be proofed for dark/light contrast and for legibility, especially when several styles or colors of cards are interfiled.

"Proofing" Products

Computer output products used to validate the data in the system must be more carefully checked for content as the computer does not simply copy previously arranged data. These products may display data record-by-record, and/or exploded by catalog section, much as the final page will appear. The first is used to validate record content in itself; the latter is used to validate interfiling of the exploded records, cross-references, and the production of running headings.

Videocomp pages are also proofing products inasmuch as they must be checked for the representation of characters not available in the computer printouts, and for errors not noted in the uni-font computer proofing products. The videocomp pages also serve as a sample of the quality of reproduction that can be anticipated.

Computer Tape Files

A further consideration in the computer production of a book catalog are the digitized files of the library's bibliographic data from which the products are derived. These files are normally considered the property of the library and, along with their formats, should be available to the library at any time, especially when a contract is up for rebid or change of vendor. These files should be available to the library for the cost of the tape and copying time, plus a small fee. Other formats of the data base may be requested by the library, again at a cost commensurate with the effort required to produce the product.

Communication

A final but important aspect of the relationship between the library and the book catalog producer is a good channel of communication. Apart from the contract itself, an amicable relationship should be established and nurtured between the two parties producing the book catalog. Contact persons and telephone numbers should be established, and communication should be frequent. Communication is all the more essential on an initial contract to assure mutual understanding of progress or lack of it. A procedures manual should be furnished to the library by the contractor when the library performs any of the work. If the book catalog production involves a computer, the manual should explain in some detail the workings of the computer system, as well as the coding, keying, correction routines, and other procedures.

Annotated Bibliography

Allison, Scott. "Book Catalogs: Pros and Cons." In *Reader in Technical Services,* edited by Edmond L. Applebaum, pp. 101–16. Washington, D.C.: NCR Microcard Editions, 1973.

  Presents a brief historical overview and covers information needed for decision making on book catalogs: pros, cons, costs, and conclusions. Describes card and book catalogs as an interim method of bibliographic storage and control prior to computer storage of bibliographic information in an on-line mode.

American Library Association. Resources and Technical Services Division. Book Catalogs Committee. "Book Form Catalogs: a Listing Compiled from Questionnaires Submitted to the Book Catalogs Directory Subcommittee, ALA, 1968." *Library Resources and Technical Services* 14:341–54 (1970).

  A listing of active book form catalogs of some 134 institutions responding to a questionnaire. Contains information on update patterns, reissue cycle, arrangement and format, costs, year of first issue, and production methods.

Automated Data Services. "Book Catalogs for the State Library of Oregon." *LARC Reports.* v.1, issue 1, no. 5 (April 1968). 2 p.

  A brief outline of the steps used for converting the card catalog of the library to a computer-produced book catalog: microfilming, coding, and sequential numbering, editing for computer input, keypunching, and computer printing.

Avedon, Dan M. *Fundamentals of Computer Output Microfilm.* National Microfilm Assn., 1974.

  Provides an introduction to COM (Computer Output Microfilm), including its advantages and applications, formats and operational considerations. Includes a glossary of terms.

Baker, Alfred W.; Boots, Frederick; and Pultz, Donald. *Automation at the Fairfax County Virginia Library System.* Tempe, Ariz.: LARC Assn., 1975. 52 p. (Computerized cataloging systems series, v.1, issue 2).

  Case study of a county library system's development and use of a book catalog. Includes reasons for converting from a card catalog, description of production methods selected, some procedures used, user aids developed, and sample pages of the final product.

Barnholdt, B. "Computerization of the UDC Classed Library Catalogue of Denmark's Danske Bibliotek, Copenhagen," *Libri* 21:234–45 (1971).

Describes the library's computerized catalog system, which provides complete catalogs in book form, easily reproduced and updated to its many branches throughout Denmark. Illustrated by worksheets for data recording and a system flow chart.

Bolef, Doris et al. "Mechanization of Library Procedures in the Medium-Sized Medical Library: Suspension of Computer Catalog." *Medical Library Association Bulletin* 57:264–66 (July 1969).

A trial period of using only a computer printed book catalog (which had formerly been used to supplement the card catalog) proved that the system in operation was inadequate. Reasons why the old system failed are given, and the plans for a new system are discussed.

Bowden, Virginia M., and Miller, Ruby B. "MARCIVE: a Cooperative Automated Library System." *Journal of Library Automation* 7:183–200 (Sept. 1974).

MARCIVE is a batch computer system utilizing both MARC tapes and local cataloging to provide catalog cards, book catalogs, and selective bibliographies for five academic libraries in San Antonio, Texas. The development of the system is outlined and procedures are described.

Brandhorst, Wesley T. *Book Catalogs; Selected References.* Bethesda, Md.: Leasco Systems and Research Corp., 1969. 13 p.

There are 116 citations for the years 1960–69 covering the following aspects of book catalogs: preparation, preservation and maintenance, economics and costs, mechanization, conversion to machine-readable form, book vs. card catalogs, and the computerized catalog.

Buckland, Lawrence F. "Mechanized Concepts of Library Catalog Production; a Comparative Study of IBM Procedures Reported by IBM Technical Publications Department and a Report Prepared for the Council on Library Resources by Lawrence F. Buckland." *LARC Reports,* v. 1, issue 1, no. 4 (April 1968). 18 p.

A comparative review of the procedures recommended in two reports for catalog data manuscript preparation, machine encoding, and conversion processing.

Buckland, Lawrence F. et al. *Final Report, Phase I: Survey of Automated Library Systems.* Maynard, Mass.: Inforonics, 1973. 182 p.

Tabulates and analyzes collected data on automated systems in use in twenty-seven libraries in this country. At least seven of the libraries produce book catalogs in some form, and this book provides specific information on production equipment and methods used.

Cartwright, Kelly L. "Automated Production of Book Catalogs." In *Library Automation: a State of the Art Review*. Papers presented at the Preconference Institute on Library Automation, San Francisco, 1967, pp. 55–78. Chicago: American Library Assn., 1969.

Automated production methods (including pitfalls) and processing of book catalogs, keyboarding, editing, creation of multiple entries, sorting, and merging new entries into file. Provides twenty sample pages of various types of book catalogs.

———. "Mechanization and Library Filing Rules." *Advances in Librarianship* 1:59–94 (1970).

Comprehensive account of the problems that filing rules present to the system designer who is attempting to incorporate a filing subsystem into mechanized catalog production. Examines the purpose of filing rules, criteria for their determination and evaluation, and discusses the technique and methods of developing filing systems for computer production of bibliographic tools. Includes a review of work that has actually been done in the area of system design and implementation.

Cayless, C.F., and Potts, Hilary. *Bibliography of Library Automation, 1964–1967*. London: Council of the British National Bibliography, 1968. 107 p.

Of the 406 annotated citations relating to library automation for the period covered, some 45 relate to book catalogs and their production, covering such subjects as book catalogs, data analysis and conversion projects, filing, and centralized catalogs.

Chapin, Richard E, and Pretzer, Dale H. "Comprehensive Costs of Converting Shelf List Records to Machine Readable Form," *Journal of Library Automation* 1:66–74 (March 1968).

Use of a service bureau to convert a shelflist to machine-readable form at Michigan State University. Compares costs of this method with trial keypunching and papertape typewriting costs in-house. Recommends use of a service bureau over other methods.

Dataflow Systems, Inc. *An Introduction to COM (Computer Output Microfilm)*. Rev. ed., Bethesda, Md.: Dataflow Systems, Inc., 1975.

Contains useful information about COM, its uses, sample costs, detailed specifications and systems descriptions of some representative COM devices. Includes a good eighty-item bibliography on micrographics.

DeGennaro, Richard. "Harvard University's Widener Library Shelflist Conversion and Publication Program," *College and Research Libraries* 31:318–31 (Sept. 1970).

Conversion of the Harvard Widener Library shelflist to produce a machine-readable form of the library's holdings, with final computer printout in multiple copies available to many readers. Discusses various potential uses of a machine readable data base. Sample pages of the printout included.

Dolby, J.L., and Forsyth, V.J. "An Analysis of Cost Factors in Maintaining and Updating Card Catalogs." *Journal of Library Automation* 2:219–41 (Dec. 1969).

Enumerates and compares costs of manual and computerized catalogs; includes conversion, cataloging, card processing, and card catalog costs. Brief discussion of relative advantages between book and card catalogs. Concludes that costs of manual and automated methods are basically the same for short entries, but that there is substantial economic advantage for automated methods in full entries.

Dolby, J.L.; Forsyth, V.J.; and Resnikoff, H.L. *Computerized Library Catalogs: Their Growth, Costs, and Utility.* Cambridge, Mass.: M.I.T. Pr., 1969. 164 p.

Main emphasis is on (1) cost factors in automation of library catalogs including computer hardware and programming, conversion of retrospective and current catalog files, and costs to the user; (2) utility of automated catalogs. Special sections on the influence of typography costs on printed catalog costs, and the use of efficient automatic error detection procedures in processing bibliographic records. Primary conclusion reached is that "mechanization of the cataloging function is not only desirable and necessary, but also inevitable."

Dougherty, Richard M., and Stephens, James G. *Investigation concerning the Modification of the University of Illinois Computerized Serials Book Catalog to Achieve an Operative System at the University of Colorado Libraries.* Boulder: Univ. of Colorado Library, 1968. 59 p.

Describes some of the difficulties of using another library's system, mainly because of lack of standardization, both bibliographic and in the scope of the data bases. Concludes the feasibility of adapting such a system under certain circumstances, and with difficulty. Recommends active participation of staff in planning as being of paramount importance.

Feinberg, Hilda. "Sample Book Catalogs and their Characteristics." In Maurice F. Tauber and Hilda Feinberg, *Book Catalogs,* pp. 381–511. Metuchen, N.J.: Scarecrow, 1971.

Sample pages with some information about the methods used to produce them from book catalogs of thirty-two libraries in the United States.

Freedman, Maurice J. "Cataloging Systems: 1973 Applications Status." In *Library Automation; a State of the Art Review,* edited by Susan Martin, pp. 56–86. Chicago: American Library Assn., 1974.

A general review of automation and cataloging, which includes much information about several recently developed systems at large libraries which have book catalogs as their final product, particularly Stanford's BALLOT-SPIRES project, New York Public Library's book catalog, University of California Union Supplement, and Hennepin County Library book catalog.

French, Thomas. "Conversion of Library Card Catalogues." *Program* 5:41–65 (May 1971).

A survey of some means, mostly photographic or mechanized, of converting a large catalog to book form. Details given are for the Birmingham University catalogs, Birmingham, England. Includes extensive bibliography (fifty-eight items) on conversion of card catalogs.

Frota, Lia M. de A., and Nunes, Renaldo P. "Automation of Library Catalogs: Catalog Automation of the Navy Library." In LARC Association, *Survey of Automated Activities in the Libraries of Mexico, Central America and South America,* pp. 26–46. Tempe, Ariz., 1972.

Details Brazilian Ministry of the Navy Library project to computerize their program, updating, back-up, integration with other systems, and training of personnel. Numerous figures, flow chart, samples of input format and keypunch cards, book catalog pages.

Gibson, Liz. "BIBCON; a General Purpose Software System for MARC-based Book Catalog Production." *Journal of Library Automation* 6:237–56 (Dec. 1973).

Designed for use on IBM 360 system equipment, BIBCON performs two basic functions: (1) it creates MARC structured bibliographic records from untagged input data and (2) it produces from these records page image output for book catalogs in a variety of formats, by line printer, photocomposition, or computer-output-microfilm. Detailed description of programs with sample pages.

Gildenberg, Robert F. *Computer-Output-Microfilm Systems.* Los Angeles: Melville Pub. Co., 1974. 199 p.

Describes design, installation, and evaluation of computer-output-microfilm (COM) systems. Provides a systematic approach to a COM study including hardware and software considerations, choice of COM service bureau, creation of in-house COM production facilities, and evaluation of installed systems. Shows how COM can be successfully combined with other types of systems.

Grosch, Audrey N. "The Minnesota Union List of Serials." *Journal of Library Automation* 6:167–81 (Sept. 1973).

Describes development of a MARC serials format union catalog of serials. Preliminary edition, August 1972, contains over 37,000 main entries in 1,566 text pages produced through photocomposition in News Gothic typefont using the full MARC character set. Conceptualization and scope of the system as well as its design, data conversion, computer and programming support, photocomposition, costs, and problems are discussed.

Harris, Jessica L., and Hines, Theodore C. "The Mechanization of the Filing Rules for Library Catalogs: Dictionary or Divided." *Library Resources and Technical Services* 14:502–16 (Fall 1970).

Emphasizes significance of rigorous entry formatting for machine filing of computer produced bibliographic tools (including book catalogs). Reports a study of computer filing done at Columbia University School of Library Service which utilized the arrangement possibilities of the computer and careful format design to considerable advantage.

Henderson, James W., and Rosenthal, Joseph A. *Library Catalogs: their Preservation and Maintenance by Photographic and Automated Techniques.* Cambridge, Mass.: MIT Pr., 1968. 267 p.

A study of the New York Public Library catalog citing recommendations for producing a book catalog employing an automated system for new cataloging. Conversion of older catalog records to a book format would be accomplished photographically. Includes cost data on book catalogs, photographic techniques, and computer production. Retrospective catalog would be reproduced by photographic methods in book form.

International Business Machines Corp. *Library Automation: Computer Produced Book Catalog.* White Plains, N.Y.: IBM, 1969. 41 p.

General discussion of book catalog production with main emphasis on computer systems. Covers input devices and work forms; programs and processing (maintenance, editing, filing); schedules; reproduction; economics; and special catalogs.

Jeffreys, Alan E. *The Conversion of the Catalogue into Machine Readable Form.* Newcastle upon Tyne: Oriel Pr., 1972. 95 p.

A British report describing a joint project between the Great Britain Office of Scientific and Technical Information and the University of Newcastle upon Tyne. Gives detailed account of processing (keypunching data from catalog cards without editing onto paper tape) and stages of converting 260,000 catalog cards of the University's author catalog.

John Shaw Associates. "Introduction to a Feasibility Study on Library Book Catalogs." *LARC Reports,* v.1, issue 1, no. 8 (April 1968). 5 p.

Discusses the problems of standardization of cataloging practices among libraries so that central cataloging and production of book catalogs will be cost effective. Aimed mainly at commercial firms entering the field.

Johnson, Richard D. "A Book Catalog at Stanford." *Journal of Library Automation* 1:13–50 (March 1968).

A detailed, comprehensive description of the system designed to produce the Stanford Undergraduate Library book catalog, with copies for many locations on campus; from conversion of cataloging information into machine-readable form, through computer programs and printing, to the final format. Interesting information given about the decision making processes involved. Some costs, sample pages, and conclusions.

Jolloffe, N.W. "Some Problems of Maintaining a Computer Edition of the General Catalogue of Printed Books," *Libri* 21:109–17 (1971).

Paper concerned with the techniques used to maintain a legible form of the British Museum's General Catalogue. It assumes that the catalog exists in machine-readable form and examines problems of cumulation, file organization, and filing.

Kennedy, John P. "Automating Library Cataloging." In *Proceedings of the Librarianship Training Institute, Louisiana Tech University, June 14–28, 1970,* pp. 136–63, Ruston, La.: Prescott Library Pub., 1971.

Describes the Georgia Tech Library automation project in rather detailed fashion, including book catalog production. Covers costs, includes flowcharts.

———. "Local MARC Project: the Georgia Tech Library," In *Proceedings of the 1968 Clinic on Library Applications of Data Processing,* edited by Dewey E. Carroll, pp. 199–215. Urbana: Univ. of Illinois, 1969.

Georgia Tech Library's use of MARC in the MARC Pilot Project I, 1966–67, to produce a book catalog. Includes description of the library system, reasons for decision to go to book form, bibliographic information included, format selected, production methods used, plans for future cumulations. Some costs, sample flowcharts, problems, and solutions are given.

Kieffer, P. "Book Catalog: To Have or Not to Have," *Library Re-*

sources and Technical Services 15:290–99 (Summer 1971).

Twenty-nine questions to be asked before deciding on a book catalog, with comments based on the experience of the Baltimore County Public Library in publishing its computer produced catalog. (Also issued as chapter in Tauber, Maurice, *Book Catalogs,* below.)

Kountz, John C. "BIBLIOS Revisited." *Journal of Library Automation* 5:63–86 (June 1972).

Orange County Public Library's earlier reports on its BIBLIOS system are updated to include two recently completed modules: book catalog and circulation control. Details about the modules, as well as documentation on development and operation costs.

———. "Cost Comparison of Computer Versus Manual Catalog Maintenance." *Journal of Library Automation* 1:159–77 (Sept. 1968).

Analyzes costs of the two types of systems (manual card catalog and computer produced book catalog) at Orange County Public Library. Gives details of methods used to arrive at costs given, as well as a breakdown of costs for both the original product and for supplements. Cautions that these are for an operating system with relatively large number of branches.

LARC Association. "Comparative Approaches to Library Book Catalog Production." LARC Reports, v.1, issue 1, no. 7 (April 1968). 13 p.

Brief discussion of three technical methods for producing book catalogs: (1) keypunched cards—unit record system, (2) cardwriter method, (3) preparing cataloged data in machine form. Some cost figures and sample pages included.

———. "Forum." *LARC Reports,* v.1, issue 2, no. 20 (July 1968). 7 p.

Three short papers on different points to consider when producing a book catalog: (1) commercial production, (2) importance of typography and composition to final product, (3) effectiveness and costs of cross-referencing subject headings.

———. "Library Automation at the New York Public Library and the Association of New York Libraries for Technical Services." *LARC Reports,* v.3, issue 3 (Fall 1970). 103 p.

The New York Public Library effort, which concentrated on the development of photocomposed book catalogs, is comprehensively covered in a series of articles by its staff; liberally illustrated with charts, diagrams, tables, and photographs.

LARC Association. "Phototypeset Output Versus Computer Print-Out in Book Catalog Production." *LARC Reports*, v.1, issue 2, no. 13 (July 1968). 13 p.

Comparative cost studies of two methods of book catalog production. Describes the methods used to obtain the cost figures from four commercial firms operating under fixed specifications.

―――. "Sample Pages of Library Book Catalogs," *LARC Reports,* v.1, issue 1, no. 9 (April 1968). 19 p.

Sample pages from the book catalogs of sixteen libraries are reproduced.

―――. "The Third Conversion of Book Catalogs for the Los Angeles County Library." *LARC Reports,* v.1, issue 1, no. 2 (April 1968). 23 p.

Divided into two parts: (1) the library's invitation to bid on the production of their book catalogs, third conversion, describing the needs of the system in detail; (2) two critical comments on the bid invitation which point out a need to outline cataloging control factors which drastically affect costs.

Linklater, W. "Catalogues in Bookform: Comparative Production Costs," *LASIE* 4:16–24 (Nov. 1973).

Australian article on costs of three forms of book catalogs. Calculations of unit and/or comparison costs given for (a) use of line printer on multiple part stationery, (b) offset printing from photoreduced plates taken from line printed originals, (c) offset printing from printing plates produced via photocomposition directly from magnetic tape.

MacQuarrie, Catherine. "Automated Library Procedures Used by Professional Library Services," *LARC Reports,* v.1, issue 2, no. 18 (July 1968). 13 p.

Outlines methods and procedures used by a commercial firm to provide catalog cards and book catalogs for material it processes and sells.

Mahood, Ramona M. "Book Catalogs: Present and Future." *Southeastern Librarian* 20:83–92 (Summer 1970).

Discusses and briefly compares special features of book catalogs at various libraries with regard to form and amount of information supplied, methods of production, general costs, user acceptance, and conclusions. Includes a brief history of book catalogs and a discussion of card versus book catalogs.

Malinconico, S. Michael, and Rizzolo, James A. "The New York Public Library Automated Book Catalog Subsystem." *Journal of Library Automation* 6:3–36 (March 1973).

Production of a photocomposed book catalog led to the development of a comprehensive automated bibliographic control system at NYPL. Its unique feature is an automated authority system which controls all established entries and their cross-reference structure. Detailed account of the design, programming, and methods of producing cumulations and supplements. Includes samples of page layout, full main and condensed added entries, and a discussion of the highly sophisticated machine-filing algorithms.

Mason, Charlene. "Bibliography of Library Automation," *ALA Bulletin* 63:1117–34 (Sept. 1969).

Selected bibliography limited to material in journal literature, trade publications, and technical reports in English, dated 1967 and 1968. Updates the earlier McCune and Salmon bibliography on the subject. Has sections on Cataloging (Book catalogs, bibliographics, and lists) and on Cataloging (Conversion of bibliographic records).

Massonneau, Suzanne. "Main Entry and the Book Catalog," *Library Resources and Technical Services* 15:499–512 (Fall 1971).

Discusses the functions of the main entry in book catalog structure—some areas where it is a continuing necessity and others where it is not. Excerpts from Stanford University book catalog provide illustrations for these points. The conclusion is that elimination of portions of the cataloging description should only be done after careful consideration.

Miele, Anthony W. "The Illinois State Library Microfilm Automated Catalog (IMAC)," *Illinois Libraries* 54:199–202 (March 1972).

Brief account of the conversion of the library's retrospective catalog into microfilm and a description of IMAC. Includes cost figures and discusses method of updating the microfilm catalog on a quarterly basis.

Morse, Grant W. *Filing Rules, a Three-Way Divided Catalog.* Hamden, Conn.: Linnet Books, 1971. 121 p.

Presents a new set of filing rules intended to meet more adequately the needs of a three-way divided card catalog, a book catalog, indexes, and directories. Arrangement is strictly alphabetical, disregarding punctuation and form headings.

Patrinostro, Frank, ed. *World Survey Series.* Tempe, Ariz.: LARC Assn., 1971–72. 4 v.

A survey of automated activities in the libraries of the world. Each reporting library describes its projects and specifies their exact status. Includes a variety of information: for example, whether project is done by library, experiences in obtaining machine time, programming language used. Automation coordinator's name is given in each case.

Phillips, Brian F. "The Computer-Produced Map Catalog: Some Considerations and a Look at Operating Systems." *Drexel Library Quarterly* 9:71–78 (Oct. 1973).

Lists a number of computer produced map catalogs, some in book form, and describes their design and method of production. Brief explanation of MARC II format for maps in included.

Phillips, Brian, and Rogers, Gary. "Simon Fraser University Computer Produced Map Catalogue." *Journal of Library Automation* 2:105–15 (1969).

An automated book catalog was produced for a previously uncataloged map collection by area and subject. An IBM 360/50 computer and magnetic tape were used. Article describes production procedures and format and gives limited cost data.

Piternick, George. "Machine and Cataloging." In *Advances in Librarianship,* edited by Melvin J. Voigt, v.1., pp. 1–35. New York: Academic Pr., 1970.

A review of developments in machines and their implications for cataloging and catalogs. Describes book catalogs in ten United States libraries (format, content, and use) and discusses advantages and disadvantages of both book and card catalogs, outlining situations where each is preferable.

Pulsifer, Josephine S. "MARC Book Catalog Production in Washington State." In *Proceedings of the 1970 Clinic on Library Applications of Data Processing: MARC Uses and Users,* edited by Kathryn Luther Henderson, pp. 53–65. Urbana: Univ. of Illinois, 1971.

Describes the use of MARC as a basis for coordinating records from many libraries in the Washington State Library system to produce a union book catalog. The catalog is used to facilitate library cooperation by making it possible for the participating libraries to share resources.

Rather, John C. "Filing Arrangement in the Library of Congress Catalogs." *Library Resources and Technical Services* 16:240–61 (Spring 1972).

Examines the functions of large bibliographic files, the interaction between users and catalogs, and principles for simplification of filing arrangement. Includes abridged version of the new Library of Congress filing rules with examples. Although primarily designed for card catalogs, the proposed filing rules are applicable to machine filing in computer produced book catalogs.

Roberts, Edward Graham, and Kennedy, John P. "The Georgia Tech Library's Microfiche Catalog." *Journal of Micrographics* 6:245–51 (July 1973).

Describes creation of a microfiche catalog, consisting of a basic file of cataloged materials up to September 1971 and bi-monthly supplements produced by COM. Basic catalog is divided into author-title, subject, and serial sections; the supplements have separate author and title sections. Includes some cost figures and illustrations of density of fiche entries.

Sacco, Concetta N. "Book Catalog Use Study." *Reference Quarterly* 12:259–66 (Spring 1973)

Report of a small sample study of book catalog use in two libraries (District Center Library, West Chester, Pa., and Forest Park Community College Library, St. Louis, Mo.). Three hundred seventy book catalog users were interviewed to determine success or failure rate, whether specific or subject search was undertaken, title or author search if specific, amount and types of bibliographic data needed. General conclusions were reached. One result indicated that users are generally favorable toward book catalogs.

Schwartz, Shula, and DiPietro, Lawrence. "A Micromation Catalog of Library Holdings." *Texas Library Journal* (Summer, 1970).

Describes the development and use of a microfilm catalog at El Centro College, Dallas, Texas.

Scott, Jack W. "An Integrated Computer Based Technical Processing System in a Small College Library," *Journal of Library Automation* 1:149–58 (June 1968).

Report of a functioning technical processing system in a two-year community college utilizing flexowriter with punch card control, IBM keypunch, and IBM 1440 computer to produce acquisition and catalog files, including a book form catalog.

Simmons, P.A. "An Analysis of Bibliographic Data Conversion Costs." *Library Resources and Technical Services* 12:296–311 (Summer 1968).

Cost studies done on the MARC Pilot Project to determine data conversion costs. Discusses the establishment of realistic standards. Describes procedures in detail with a breakdown of costs for each step in processing MARC records.

Stultz, George B. "Automating the Library Operations of the Idaho Nuclear Corporation." *LARC Reports,* v.1, issue 3, nos. 21–28 (Sept. 1968). 132 p.

Library procedures at the Idaho Nuclear Corporation using electronic data processing equipment are fully described. Chapter 2 (report no. 22) deals specifically with the book lists and printed catalog. Includes procedural methods, with specific information about the computer program, and sample pages of the final product.

Tauber, Maurice F., and Feinberg, Hilda. *Book Catalogs.* Metuchen, N.J.: Scarecrow, 1971. 572 p.

A selection of twenty-eight papers providing some description of

......is developing in book catalogs in academic, special, county, public, and school libraries. Many papers cover specific problems encountered such as format, costs, methodology, and usefulness, and provide examples and illustrations.

————— "Book Catalogs." In Conrad H. Rawski, *Toward a Theory of Librarianship,* pp. 350–77. Metuchen, N.J.: Scarecrow, 1973.

Discusses book catalogs: (1) brief history and background information, (2) methods of production, (3) format, (4) costs, (5) advantages and disadvantages, (6) future possibilities. Overlaps to some extent with their *Book Catalogs.*

Tinker, Lynne. *An Annotated Bibliography of Library Automation, 1968–1972.* London: Aslib, 1973. 85 p.

Includes many articles relating to book catalogs, both directly and indirectly.

Tucker, C.J. "A Comparison of the Production Costs of Different Physical Forms of Catalogue Output." *Program* 8:59–75 (April 1974).

Compares the cost of producing different physical forms of catalogs with output from a bibliographic data base, including line-printer hard copy, COM for offset/litho printing, magnetic tape for phototypesetting, 16–mm microfilm, microfiche, and ultrafiche. A British publication.

Waldron, Helen J. *Book Catalogs: a Survey of the Literature on Costs.* Santa Monica, Calif.: Rand Corp., 1971. 26 p.

Advantages and disadvantages of both card and book catalogs are considered. Costs are drawn from the existing literature and compared for various kinds of techniques and for various parts of the production. Conclusion reached is that it is not economically sound to plan on a book catalog unless many copies are required or high cost can be justified. Extensive annotated bibliography included.

West, Martha W.; Koch, Rowena; and Butler, Brett. "Computer Filing vs. ALA Filing Rules." *California Librarian* 34:47–56 (April 1973).

Discussion of the major differences between ALA filing rules and the standard computer merge/sort program, particularly for title entries. Data source for the study is CARDSET, a microfilm cataloging service by Information Design, Inc. which produces a catalog and two indexes (Library of Congress number and title). Includes tables comparing third generation IBM computer standard collating sequence and ALA filing rules, and samples of filing position variances.

Other AᒪA *Publications of Interest to Catalogers*

ALA Rules for Filing Catalog Cards, 2d ed.
Pauline A. Seely, ed. $7.00

Detailed code for filing catalog cards covers specialized and foreign material and includes philosophical descriptive notes pertaining to filing principles and their correlation with cataloging rules. All rules and examples are based on the form in which headings and entries are made according to standard cataloging rules and practices. Designed for a dictionary card catalog, the rules also apply to divided catalogs, book catalogs, and indexes. For all libraries. Glossary, bibliography, index.

ALA Rules for Filing Catalog Cards, 2d ed., abridged
Pauline A. Seeley, ed. $2.50

Presents the same basic rules as the unabridged edition but omits most of the specialized and explanatory material.

Catalog Card Reproduction:
Report on a Study Conducted by George Fry & Associates.
LTP Publication No. 9 $9.00

Describes and analyzes thirteen processes for obtaining or reproducing catalog cards in the library. Costs of equipment, materials, and staff time are shown for all processes.

Cataloging U.S.A.
Paul S. Dunkin $6.00

A basic and fundamental examination of cataloging theory, principles, and practice as they have developed in the United States. Scrutinizing cataloging theory in the light of logic, history, and practical results, this penetrating, spritely commentary explores the "why" rather than the "how" of cataloging.

Library Automation: The State of the Art II
Susan K. Martin and Brett Butler, eds. $7.50

These preconference proceedings evaluate the advances of library automation since 1968. Leaders in the field of library automation provide a valuable perspective on where we are today, how we got there, and what we can expect by 1980 in papers discussing computer technology, user services, cataloging systems, acquisitions systems, systems personnel, innovative strategies, and predictions for the future. Includes a bibliography on library automation compiled by Martha W. West.

Reprographic Services in Libraries: Organization and Administration
LTP Publication No. 19.
Charles G. LaHood, Jr., and Robert C. Sullivan $4.50

This manual has been produced to assist librarians in initiating a reprographic service for patrons as well as in organizing, managing, and maintaining existing services. Reprography includes the widest possible combination of documentary reproduction services that may be offered in a library—photocopying, photography, and microphotography. The emphasis in this LTP publication is on general guidelines and policy considerations rather than on technical processes or detailed laboratory procedures.

All Published by

AMERICAN LIBRARY ASSOCIATION
50 East Huron Street, Chicago, Illinois 60611

8389-31